CW00548356

Cambridgeshire Fens

– Landscapes and Legends –

Text by Trevor Bevis

Paintings by Malcolm Allen

Cottage Publications

First published by Cottage Publications,
an imprint of Laurel Cottage Ltd.
Donaghadee, N. Ireland 2010.
Copyrights Reserved.
© Illustrations by Malcolm Allen 2010.
© Text by Trevor Bevis 2010.
All rights reserved.
No part of this book may be reproduced or stored on any media
without the express written permission of the publishers.
Design & origination in Northern Ireland.
Printed & bound in China.
ISBN 978 1 900935 86 9

The Author

Trevor Bevis was born at Pinchbeck, Lincolnshire in 1930 and moved to March at the outbreak of the Second World War, where he began an apprenticeship as a journalist for a firm publishing provincial newspapers. He later became a printer.

Trevor has always been interested in the history of East Anglia, and especially the Fens, and he has written and published well over 100 books about almost every town south of Boston, and the Fens in general.

His other interests include campanology, but he has recently retired from this hobby. Trevor enjoys producing line drawings and photography, which he combines with visits to hundreds of churches and cathedrals where, in the past, he joined local bell ringers. He is a keen cyclist, and many of the trips to churches were undertaken by this mode of transport, with a notebook and pen tucked in his pocket to record the experiences. He and his wife, June, have three children and six grandchildren.

The Artist

Malcolm Allen's love of the fenland landscape came from an early age. The son of a Fenland farmer, he always had a strong affinity with the area, its flatness, large sky, history, wildlife and agriculture.

He has been painting for over thirty years and, with no formal art training, is primarily self taught. The Fens are an integral part of his life and living so close, many of his works are of this area. His works are predominantly watercolour, but he will use other media depending on the inspiration of the moment. With competition success he has exhibited at Oxford Castle. He exhibits extensively in East Anglia and, with several one man shows, is proud to have examples of work in private collections worldwide.

Now a retired Civil Engineer he lives in West Norfolk with his wife of forty years, Elizabeth. Their three children and four grandchildren are close by.

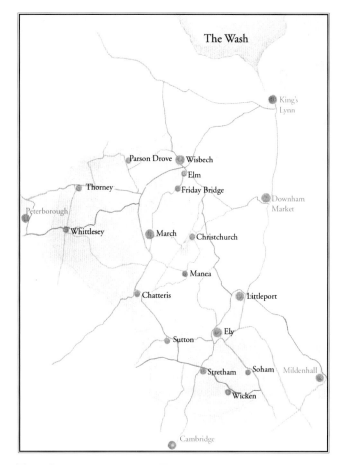

THE CAMBRIDGESHIRE FENS

Contents

The Fens: Man versus Water

The Fen district north of Cambridge comprises beds of clay, peat and gravel. The original course from east to west of the River Great Ouse indicates the termination of the Fens in these parts where the lowland gives way to higher ground. Beyond, the Fens stretch about seventy miles north into Lincolnshire and spread into west Norfolk. 'Islands', which are principally found in the Cambridgeshire Fens, rise from rocks lying beneath Oxford clay, Kimmeridge clay, and other deposits on which the towns of Ely, Chatteris, Whittlesey and March developed.

Some islands are dramatic and spectacular to approach, ranging from a metre to 24.5 metres in height; the most prominent and largest is that on which Ely and its attendant villages are situated. A part of the same island on which Haddenham, Wilburton and Stretham developed forms a high ridge overlooking the Fens towards

Cambridge. This ridge, the highest part of the island, has been called the Fen Alps.

The islands were highly favoured by religious recluses and the area became known throughout the land as The Holy Land of the English. Not only Anglo-Saxon individuals were drawn to the remoteness of the islands but bands of monks founded abbeys on the elevated areas and re-peopled places like Ely, Thorney, Ramsey and Chatteris. The islands of varying heights were natural sanctuaries for the Fen dwellers employed in wild fowling and at the numerous fisheries as well as limited agricultural work on the higher ground.

FLOODED FENS

Aerial photography has revealed that the Romans made use of semi-drained areas and cultivated crops in small fields, but things became considerably different in Anglo-Saxon times, the land having subsided and a general state of neglect prevailed. Over a course of several centuries the Fens were subjected by water incursion to rapid deterioration and became a hostile wilderness.

Covering a vast lowland area, the Fens were a dangerous, unwelcoming environment two thousand years ago. No-one in their right senses ventured from the uplands into the Fens. A hardy race, the Gyrwas (people of the water), eked out a living from an abundance of wildlife and made light of waterborne disabilities. The ague, a Fen malady, could be fatal to those unused to it. 'Fen sloggers' took it all in their stride and, after a few debilitating days, returned to their work plodding through mud and water using traditional stilts. Shallow meres linked to waterways shrank in dry seasons and spread out over the marsh to form expansive lakes in winter.

Four hundred years later, the area was raised much higher when sea embankments, built by the Romans, became neglected and salt water and fresh water spread over marsh and fen. Water-loving plants, such as willow and alder, thrived in such conditions. Before the inundation occurred oaks, birches and firs clothed the countryside. Incursion of water caused them to die and they sank into the peat only to be discovered in our own times. Estuaries silted up and natural rivers prevented from discharging into the Wash added to the hazardous nature of the Fens. The Fens transformed into an inland sump made up of silt in areas adjoining the coastline and peat in the inland areas where the small and large islands protruded above the fresh water Fens.

For centuries it was realised that the Fens held the key to intensive agricultural and horticultural production and that if the region could be drained the alluvial deposits would be richly fertile and highly productive. It would be a daunting undertaking in which the onsets of nature would strongly oppose the efforts of men.

It is not generally realised the Fens' main rivers carry water from thirteen upland counties. The Great Ouse, the Nene, the Welland and the Witham rivers flow by gravitational impulse into the Wash. The course of each river is at a higher level than the time before drainage work began making an effect. This resulted in the land, deprived of water, acting like a sponge and causing shrinkage to occur.

Men contemplated draining small tracts of Fen and transforming it into arable land. William of Malmesbury, monk and historian, wrote of his admiration of the monks of Thorney who had successfully drained their estate 'and created a veritable paradise', harvesting all kinds of fruit and finest vines. The monks cut a system of ring ditches and gravitation emptied one into another, water finally discharging into the marsh.

In about 1250 the estuary at Wisbech dramatically altered the geological nature of the southern Fens, and rivers abruptly changed courses through swampy areas. The Ouse with its outfall into the Wash became obstructed by deposits of silt and flooded the marshland, parts of which had been reclaimed. In winter the Fens were transformed into a vast area of shallow water and marsh and inflows from encompassing upland regions combined with high tides. This considerably affected towns and villages, Wisbech in particular. Water spread over reclaimed land, destroying buildings, livestock and hundreds of people perished. Many families sought sanctuary in church towers.

In the latter half of the 15th century Bishop Morton of Ely, an engineering genius, caused a leam to be cut between Guyhirn and Stanground. The leam named after him was unbanked and not deep enough; in the winter season allowing water to overflow and spread into the Fens towards March, seriously affecting the river at that town. Arthur Smiles in his book, *Lives of the Engineers* says:

> 'The bishop was the first to introduce into the district the practice of making straight cuts and artificial rivers for the purpose of more rapidly voiding

the waters of the Fens, a practice which has been extensively adopted by the engineers of the present day.'

Bishop Morton also created a lagoon at Guyhirn, its purpose to collect water from the leam when the River Nene ran at high tide. When the tide ebbed, water discharged from the lagoon and scoured the river bed forcing obstructive silt towards Wisbech and the outfall. Some farmers erected wind-engines over drains to pass water away from their fields. This had a negative effect and usually drowned neighbouring farmers' land. It was the practice to scour Fen rivers but this had little effect, the outfalls notorious for build-up of silt and throwing water back towards the fields.

Draining the Fens

Drainage in the Fens was – and still is – an extremely expensive operation. Anciently each Fen parish was obliged to contribute financially and physically towards the maintenance of drains and embankments. Drainage experiments in the 16th century were carried out on the basis of trial and error. It was largely a private undertaking and there was no clear idea of how drainage schemes should work and certainly no co-ordination between individuals. Inspiration derived from margins of success observed in the drainage of small tracts of Fen and crops grown on emergent soil. It was reasoned that if small areas of fen could be transformed into agricultural and grazing areas it was feasible to consider a far greater scheme for excluding and controlling water affecting in excess of 100,000 acres of fen. Compounded errors made by abbots, bishops and farmers inspired the so-called Gentlemen Adventurers – mainly capitalists – to think of the impossible. Accordingly an Act was passed for the reclamation of thousands of acres of fen in north Cambridgeshire.

The plan to reclaim such a vast area was regarded by many including foreign commentators as mad, an impossible undertaking and a waste of time, money and energy. The Dutchman, Sir Cornelius Vermuyden who had experienced success in planning the drainage at Hatfield Chase, a smaller fen area near Doncaster, was commissioned to submit a plan for the drainage of the Cambridgeshire Fens and outlying areas. These were accepted and he invited the Participants of the former undertaking to join him in the Cambridgeshire project. The Participants, refugees from religious persecution in France and Flanders, had suffered persistently at Hatfield, the English destroying sluices and embankments and even attacking the refugees' houses and destroying their church. In 1650 at the invitation of the

Earl of Bedford they trekked to Thorney and established a sizeable colony.

Charles I, then experiencing severe financial problems, and impressed by the Participants' work at Hatfield Chase, enthusiastically endeared himself to the scheme. Vermuyden and his supporters, the Gentlemen Adventurers, concocted ways and means to transform the drowned acres of the Isle of Ely and outlying areas of Fen into rich, productive land albeit over a lengthy period of time. The king would receive 12,000 acres and 43,000 acres were set out to finance maintenance of the work. It was envisaged that rewards would be incalculable both in crop production and financially. The remaining Fen would be allocated to individuals who had invested capital in the project. No-one could foresee the immense problems that would arise from such an undertaking.

Vermuyden has been described as a heavy-handed Adventurer in the practical prosecution of the scheme. He did, in fact, lack a degree of foresight and probably relied on his knowledge of land reclamation from the sea in the Netherlands. In the Cambridgeshire Fens he was pitched against the problem of fresh water flooding and became a victim of bitterness and envy among the natives and fellow Adventurers. Among other things he was accused of making sluices using inferior materials and taking land illegally. These accusations were probably pure fabrication. It is acknowledged that Vermuyden did make errors of judgement but it was impossible to envisage the ultimate result of such a grandiose scheme. It took more than 200 years to realise the complete drainage of the Fens and numerous improvements have been made since 1850.

The key to Vermuyden's plan lay in the area between Earith in Huntingdonshire and Denver in Norfolk, a distance of 21 miles. His original scheme included the cutting in 1630 of the Old Bedford river but, owing to this proving inadequate, the cutting of an additional river, the New Bedford, running parallel with the first mentioned, became necessary. The rivers were separated by a strip of wash land between half-a-mile and three-quarters of a mile wide. When the rivers are under pressure, water runs above lowered sections of inner embankments and floods the wash land.

Vermuyden did not guarantee that the Fens would be free of complete inundation especially in winter, a cautionary stance on his part that earned undue criticism. Farmers expected too much from the scheme, believing that from the beginning everything would be perfect. Caution was thrown to the wind and new drained land occupied prematurely. When the onslaught of winter rendered the land unworkable and pools of water drained away slowly in the growing season, scathing criticism – accompanied here and there by violence – placed the work in jeopardy. It was said that what had already been achieved was virtually ineffectual.

Charles I, motivated by potential profit, projecting himself as Chief Adventurer and saviour of the scheme, decided he would finish what the Adventurers had failed to do. The king insisted on a revised scheme from which he believed he would emerge in a sound financial position. He would take 47,000 acres and even made plans to build a royal palace at Manea in the middle of his Fenland estate. He surmised it would be called Charlemont. Vermuyden was retained as chief engineer and he prepared a revised scheme, much of which was carried out in 1650-51. A vexing problem was that of insufficient workers as no self-respecting Fenman would lift a finger to help in a project which would limit wild fowling and deplete fisheries, his livelihood. The revised scheme was finally put on a sound footing in the introduction of hundreds of Scottish and Dutch prisoners-of-war captured at the Battles of Worcester and Dunbar

and on the high seas off Portland Bill. They were set to work in cutting main drains and improving existing rivers, building sluices and raising embankments. Many, unused to the hostile, moisture-laden environment, the forays of tens of thousands of Fen stinging gnats and the debilitating ague – a Fen speciality similar to malaria – succumbed where they worked. The unfortunate men were buried on the site of their labours, namely the river banks they helped to raise. Due to the financial situation the drainage commissioners could not afford to transport the dead to sanctified graveyards and, in any case, parishioners did not want them.

PUMPING ON THE FENS

The prisoners also helped to erect wind pumps similar to windmills. These were always uneconomical and dangerous to the families that occupied them, the elements constantly ruining sails and worse, the pumps were often becalmed. About a thousand wind pumps were built in the Fens passing water from one to another, a larger one finally lifting water into a main drain. These pumps were literally allowed to collapse and, during the 19th century, brick-buildings housing steam-powered beam pumps were erected at strategic sites. Fuelled by coal and, in some instances dried peat obtained locally, these engines witnessed the complete drainage of the

Fens. They were not cheap to run. In 1851 the world's first steam-driven centrifugal pump sucked to oblivion Whittlesey Mere, the largest freshwater lake in southern England. Engines such as these were never becalmed, were reliable and worked, if necessary, for days or weeks on end. That at Stretham installed in the first half of the 19th century last worked in 1941.

At their zenith in 1750 most wind pumps were owned by farmers and worked relatively small areas, often discharging water on to neighbouring farmers' land. In 1800 about 250 remained, others abandoned through the destructive nature of the elements. Beam engines with tall chimneys were rated at between 60 and 105 horse power. The scoop wheels had a diameter of about 37 feet. One with 50 ladles lifted about 30 tons of water with each revolution.

The efficacy of Watt-type beam engines can be measured in that nineteen strategically placed units performed the work of 250 wind pumps. The beam pumps worked well and lofty smoking chimneys brought a satisfying degree of confidence to the Fens' farming community. Even so on occasions water in the main drains built up and sometimes topped the banks. Flooding was not as serious and affected a much smaller acreage. Many em-

bankments were raised in the Fens and, if a drain filled to bursting point, another embankment prevented water from spreading.

Three beam engines still exist at Stretham, Pinchbeck Marsh and Boston and are very popular with steam buffs and those interested in land drainage. An observer wrote:

> *'To the minds of those living by the side of rivers and drains of low, flat countries and accustomed to the slow practice of an agricultural life, there is a sense of power and solidity about a massive beam engine with its slowly revolving flywheel and heavy beam rising and falling, drawing a ponderous water wheel lifting a large mass of water.'*

Beam engines were gradually replaced by steam centrifugal pumps which introduced an era of greater efficiency. Vermuyden had not realised that drawing water from the Fens would cause land to shrink. This sponge-like effect created a phenomenon, embanked rivers and drains left high above land, confining water coursing by gravitational and artificial means as much as twenty feet above the drained level.

At the beginning of the First World War the Bedford Level Corporation was replaced by a number of drainage boards, members comprising individuals mainly from the farming community. An Act of Parliament in 1930 placed the entire Bedford Level under the auspices of the Ouse Catchment Board with greater responsibilities maintaining natural rivers, man-made drains and a large number of sluices. A new generation of diesel and electric powered pumps of varying capacities, some automatic, some manned, are strategically sited in the North Level, the Middle Level and the South Level areas. The first diesel pump was installed in Methwold Fen in 1913. Diesel and electric pumps have an obvious advantage and are significantly more efficient. Modern machinery starts instantly and is highly satisfactory for intermittent pumping.

An engraving on a plaque fixed to an old pumping station, *'In Fitness For The Urgent Hour'* exemplifies the preparedness of sophisticated machinery, the skilled workforce and engineers on constant vigil safeguarding the Fens. The vision of Middle Level commissioners inspired in 1930-34 the installation of one of the largest pumping stations in Europe situated above the main drain at Wiggenhall St. Germans. Massive concrete piles between 30 ft and 40 ft long, and 880 sheet steel piles were driven into the ground, forming firm support to withstand the pounding of huge diesel engines and water turbines housed in two low buildings. Two turbines were powered by electricity. A mass of concrete 15 ft thick formed foundations underpinned by 1,245 piles. Each unit powered a massive enclosed water impeller.

The droughts of 1990, 1991 and 1992 saw little action at Wiggenhall, with water in the Level being conserved for crop irrigation. After almost eighty years of use, sometimes for weeks at a time, the machinery was showing signs of wear and tear. This prompted the commissioners to provide new pumping units a short distance from the original pumps on the same drain, and the Middle Level Commissioners recently opened the new state-of-the-art pumping station to replace the old station built in 1934. The new station came live in April 2010. It has six electrically-driven pumps, each capable of discharging 18 tons of water per second against an average tide – a 40 per cent improvement on the old station. The new station has a suite of automatic modes dealing with all types of normal and emergency pumping requirements. In the event of grid failure, internal generators will provide power for the six pumps.

Of special interest is the fact that the new station can accommodate a degree of internal flooding and, in the unlikely event of this happening, the pumps will continue working, the station being the only exit point for storm water discharge from 700 square kilometres of fine agricultural and horticultural land encompassing 22,500 properties.

The new station has an envisaged life of 75 years, matching that achieved by the old station, now demolished. The new ultra modern station is clad in black with a high rise glass frontage allowing people to see the main pump hall. Costing £37.7 million, it is the largest in the United Kingdom. Described as the 'Wembley of pumping projects', it is believed to be the second largest in Europe.

This huge project illustrates the Middle Level Commissioners' and the government's recognition of the Fens' vital importance to the nation. Over a course of almost 400 years the historic lowland has superbly earned the accolade 'Bread basket of the nation'. The reclaimed land epitomises men's achievements in the face of nature in her most unforgiving mood.

Wisbech is a shade of Renaissance Bruges and Ghent, and maybe even a touch of Amsterdam. The Georgian aspect along the North Brink is nothing short of spectacular. There is even a hint of England's Bath in this self-styled capital of the Fens that caresses the eyes when strolling along the Crescent. The Crescent obtained its shape from the Norman/Tudor castle, a centre of infamous detention of intellectuals regarded as dangerous to the new Protestant State. The prisoners, including the last abbot of Westminster, languished here reputed to be the securest place after the Tower of London. It was here they initiated the 'Wisbech Stirs', great minds aspiring to overturn the Protestant movement.

Born in 1760 Thomas Clarkson, the town's renowned son, joined forces with William Wilberforce to bring about the anti-slavery law. Clarkson travelled the country seeking evidence of the horror of the slave trade, arming Wilberforce MP with details of ships involved in the terrible business. In his sonnet, Wordsworth wrote: *A great man's happiness thy zeal shall find; repose at length firm friend of human kind.'*

A hundred-and-fifty years ago the port of Wisbech enjoyed prolific sea links with continental ports, and ships from the old borough even sailed to America. The 1800s were the peak for Wisbech and its sea-faring am-bitions highlighted by its own eminent ship owner, Richard Young. He introduced screw steamers to his fleet, a credible milestone considering Wisbech's inland port was 14 miles from the sea and had to contend with rivals Boston and King's Lynn. Nowadays the port is attractively set out as a harbour for private yachts and cruisers.

Wisbech comes into its own in summer with its well-known Rose Fair raising funds for the parish church, a commodious building with a double-nave dating traditionally to 1111. The bell tower, built in the first half of the sixteenth century, is one of the finest in Cambridgeshire.

The Crescent

WISBECH

Malcolm D.Allen

Wisbech is a slight reflection of Georgian Bath. At Wisbech the Georgians introduced their elegant style of architecture in good measure as can be seen in the Crescent built on the site of the Norman/Tudor castle, and on the North Brink reflected in the tidal River Nene. Peckover House, a fine Georgian edifice cared for by the National Trust, has an orangery and beautiful gardens.

Joseph Medworth, a Wisbech bricklayer, who made a fortune in London, purchased Wisbech castle to build the existing house on the site. He surrounded it with houses typical of the period. Mr Medworth wanted to make a fine road from the Crescent but envious burghers would not approve and Wisbech lost its chance of becoming the Cheltenham of East Anglia.

Medworth's house faces Museum Square dominated by the Wisbech and Fenland Museum. The building contains an impressive number of relics from the Fens and further afield including objects once owned by Charles Dickens.

Overlooking the bridge, the Clarkson Memorial honours Thomas Clarkson, instigator of the anti-slavery movement. Beyond the bridge is the Old Market and the famous North Brink with its handsome Georgian and Victorian houses. The cemetery near The Friends'

Meeting House keeps a Royal link – here was buried Lady Jane, said to be the illegitimate daughter of James II. After touring royal courts abroad she ran away and came to Wisbech where she worked as a reaper. Eventually Jane became known as the Queen of the Reapers. She lived in a basement near the Old Market and made fine lace which she sold on the New Market Place. One day a fine coach drew up to the Rose and Crown inn and Jane recognised it as belonging to a nobleman who was looking for her on behalf of her father. She hurriedly packed up her stall and fled to her basement, becoming a semi-recluse teaching Latin and Greek. When walking in the cemetery she swooned and told her companion that spot would be her burial place.

North Brink

WISBECH

A National Trust property, Peckover House overlooks the river flowing between the North and South Brinks flanked by elegant Georgian buildings. The Brinks were the place to live in the influential 18th and 19th centuries; several famous Wisbechians and even the young Princess Victoria enjoyed strolling along North Brink to admire its architecture, and Peckover House is one of the splendid sights of Wisbech. Built in 1722, it is a stately residence, typical of the upstairs-downstairs era. Visitors experience the opulence and dignity of an age which put the Great in Britain. Rooms are set out in typical 18th and 19th century style, and if that is not enough, at the rear of the house are delightful gardens which, in appropriate seasons, are a mass of colour. There is also an orangery.

In the reign of George II this opulent building, then Bank House, was owned by a Baronet of the Southwell family. The Lady of the family desired to adorn it sumptuously but her husband considered it too expensive. She asked her father, a wealthy and liberal man, to help, and he sent her several thousand pounds to enable her to make the alterations.

Peckover House underwent a few changes under its wealthy owners and extensions included a library containing rare manuscripts. A second library with fine carvings was added later. The Friends' (Quakers) burial ground is nearby, and here is buried Jane Stuart, a daughter of James II. She lived for a time at Wisbech and joined the Society of Friends.

Jonathan Peckover, native of Fakenham who moved to Wisbech in 1777 founded a bank which was opened in High Street, Wisbech. It was so successful it removed to a building on North Brink adjoining Bank House. The Peckovers, an eminent family held in high esteem at Wisbech and in the neighbourhood, were highly beneficent to the town. The banking firm then known as Gurney, Birkbeck, Barclay and Buxton eventually became known as Barclay and Co.

An interesting story relates to the Peckovers. At one time, a run on the pound caused panic in the country. Ever resourceful Mr Peckover dispatched a carriage to London, so the story goes, and obtained a lot of gold coins which were displayed on bundles of paper in a barrel at the Wisbech bank. Clients, who had feared the worst, descended on the bank and, seeing the coins, felt a sense of relief that all was well at the Peckover establishment. Result? No panic! Times haven't really changed that much, have they?!

Peckover House

WISBECH

The former borough of Wisbech enjoyed the convenience of two market places, one known as the Old Market founded in Anglo-Saxon times and the New Market occupying an impressively spacious site on the opposite side of the river. The former is no longer used by marketeers.

For reasons of security it was customary in medieval times for traders to meet in an area overlooked by a castle. The market is dominated by an assortment of shops rubbing shoulders with dignified buildings and, at the southern end, the stately tower of St. Peter and St. Paul church, one of the finest campaniles in Cambridgeshire, lords over it all.

In times of yore a large shambles used by butchers stood in the centre of the market place and next to it a court house. Perhaps appropriately the town stocks were set up on the roof of this building. At least felons had a good view of what was happening around them and happily for them they were out of range of missiles, especially rotten eggs!

Wisbech miscreants experienced an awful punishment in the 1800s, suffering the indignity of being horsewhipped. Stripped to the waist the malefactor, hands tied to the tail of a horse, was led around the market place and every few steps a law officer laid into him with a raw-hide whip. At the end of the 'tour', barely able to stand, the culprit had to endure salt rubbed into his wounds. The last man to receive this punishment died of gangrene and the practice discontinued.

In Victorian times great feasts were held on the Market Place, benches and tables set out and several thousand Wisbechians, mainly the poor, sumptuously regaled. The bells rang out, flags fluttered from buildings, sharp-eyed constables patrolled and a hot air balloon floated overhead.

Those were halcyon times, Wisbech then having a thriving port and prolific ship owners dispatching sail and steam vessels to continental ports, the Baltic and occasionally to America. Sustained by incoming and outgoing trade the New Market and the Old were vital to Wisbech's prosperity.

Spring Market

WISBECH

When the Fens were declared well and truly drained, the principal crops, wheat, and in lesser quantities, barley, grew particularly well. Potatoes were later grown and Irish migrants came to the Fens in large numbers to harvest the crop. Except for its 'islands', the north part of Cambridgeshire covers about 680,000 acres of ultra-rich soil, adapting perfectly well to most crops.

A rare sight in the Fens nowadays, straw stacks are virtually relegated to history. This writer recalls every farm having a stack-yard where sheaves of wheat built into stacks awaited the attention of threshers. My grandfather, a farmer, arranged for a steam traction engine and threshing machinery to attend, and teenagers appreciated having a real steam engine present in the yard for about a week; it was hard work and farm workers were covered in dust from head to toe. I remember fondly sitting on a tractor hauling a binder which cut the wheat, tied bundles and cast them on to the ground. The sheaves were stood up to dry before being stacked.

SHADOWS AND BALES

Straw stacks attract vermin such as mice and rats, and yours truly was allowed to accompany a worker at night with a shotgun, a torch attached to the barrel, aimed at the stack. When a pair of beady eyes glinted in the light, the gun discharged. Goodbye rat! Some farmers erected nets round the base of stacks during threshing operations and vermin attempting to escape ended up in the jaws of a terrier or Jack Russell.

All this is now committed to the mists of history; old binders turn to rust on the farms and modern buildings accommodate state-of-the-art machinery including huge combine harvesters with air conditioned cabins and one man to do all the work. Even wheat has changed. Years ago, kernels developed on long straw which was susceptible to wind damage. Nowadays it is shorter and stronger.

Wheat Fields in the Fens

IN THE FENS

Malcolm Diller

This writer has never seen a single elm tree at Elm, a pretty village quite untypical of the Fens. Visitors can be forgiven for thinking they are in the heart of Suffolk. Anciently recorded as Aelm and Elum it is a well-treed place of tourist-card quality dominated by a magnificent church in the Early English style. Although heightened in the 15th century the arcaded tower is superb.

Tranquillity dwells in this evocative place which grew out of disastrous floods. It is surprising to learn that within the church in 1316 William de Petworth, priest, came to blows with his curate John Wetyng. It was usual for clergy to carry daggers beneath vestments to protect themselves against felons and the curate found himself being threatened with the blade. Apparently he had become too big for his sandals!

A previous rector declared that the old rectory is haunted by a ghostly monk named Ignatius. The monk was keeping watch on a sea bank when he fell asleep and failed to warn the village of an impending flood.

On memorable occasions Elm received the full wrath of the sea which came down to Wisbech a couple of miles away, often causing loss of life among inhabitants and leaving a swathe of destruction on a wide scale.

Urged by gale the water rushed
Upon the village still asleep.
Against Elm church it frothed and pushed
And fearful eyes from windows peep.
Man undaunted by cruel invasion
Reclaimed his faith by shaping stones,
And raised his churches to salvation
Built on silt and forebear's bones.

In the 16th century an inventive and enterprising Dutchman named Maurice erected the Fens' first wind pumps in the parish of Elm. These drainage devices were privately owned and did more harm than good. A century later hundreds of improved versions could be seen all over the Fens. At Elm when there was sufficient breeze they tended to pump water out of a field and drown neighbouring land.

All Saints Church

ELM

Malcolm D Allen

As the name implies, a bridge existed at Friday Bridge. It spanned Elm Leam, a stream coursing through the Fen from March, flowing through Elm then discharging into the river at Wisbech.

Hereabouts 'Friday' is an enigma. It is of Norse or Danish origin and relates to 'Frea', signifying a leader of men. In Norse mythology 'Freyr' was a god and, taking it further, Friday might have derived from 'Fricge' reputed to be the wife of Woden and mother of Thor, the latter relating to Thursday. So we may well ask did a Viking family settle at Friday Bridge? The Norse farmers/warriors generally favoured higher ground.

Confusing isn't it? Anyway put it in your pipe and smoke it as did the Fenmen of old in their attempts to drive away the dreaded stinging gnat so much the plague of their water-ridden lives.

Royals and anti-Royals had links with Friday Bridge. It is a typical Fen village but one thing is glaringly obvious. The substantial and lofty Victorian water tower with little aesthetic appeal lords it over the whole village. This tower is the royal link.

In past Christmases when the Queen (or King) broadcast to the nation and Commonwealth from Sandringham, the water tower surmounted with a high metal mast played an important role. The airwaves from Sandringham were intercepted at Friday Bridge and relayed to BBC London, thence to the world at large.

More than three centuries ago Oliver Cromwell passed this way with a detachment of roundhead soldiers to do battle at King's Lynn. The day was far spent and the troops weary, and the invincible Fenman, a Colonel at the time, decided to bed down at Friday Bridge. The troops passed along the track leading to Needham Hall where Cromwell was graciously received by the owner and offered a comfortable bed. "No," replied Cromwell. "How can I sleep comfortably when outside my men are bedded down in uncomfortable stables and outhouses?" He chose to sleep on a fine oak table preserved here for many years.

The author enjoyed cycling near Friday Bridge and, during World War Two, often came across groups of German and Italian prisoners-of-war encamped a mile or so away. After working on farms they enjoyed the privilege of being let out of the camp to walk along the pleasant rural lanes in the vicinity.

The Water Tower

FRIDAY BRIDGE

Malcolm D Allen

Christchurch is a small community about five miles from March. Among its mainly Victorian houses the church, screened by venerable trees, is a plain building with a simple nave and chancel. It is typical of Victorian ecclesiastical architectural design and once boasted a fine tower before cracks appeared in the wall adjoining it and the tower was taken down. Many years ago Christchurch was known as Brimstone Hill but the reason is unknown. There is nothing visibly significant here but there is one great exception.

The vicarage, formerly a Retreat surrounded by idyllic pastoral scenes and now privately owned, accommodated the Rev. and Mrs Henry Sayers. Their daughter, Dorothy Leigh, rose to the dizzy heights of fame as an internationally acclaimed novelist writing a series of murder mysteries, arguably the finest of which, *The Nine Tailors*, exceeded well over thirty editions. Her who-dunnit novels centred on Lord Peter Wimsey, a private detective in those days fictionally as famous as Morse. Lord Peter was an enthusiastic campanologist and his interests became entangled with a body that had been lodged in the belfry of Dorothy's make-believe church, Fenchurch St. Paul. It was at Christchurch vicarage in 1923 she completed her first Lord Peter novel, *Whose Body?* and she went on to create a number of serious in-depth books of great acclaim including *The Zeal Of Thy House* and *Further Papers On Dante*.

Dorothy Sayers visited Christchurch several times and walked around the village, it is said, wearing a typical Fen woman's head-scarf referred to as resembling local potato pickers' headwear! She sometimes came with her boyfriend riding a motorcycle which she far preferred to a car. Dorothy donned her colourful Oxford robes to sing in the choir, sometimes to the chagrin of her colleagues. On one occasion her beau, weary of Mr Sayers' sermon, discreetly let himself out of the church building and hared across the muddy fields to the Dun Cow to savour spirits of the other kind!

Dorothy Sayers never aspired to like the Fens though she admired the Fens' history and the stoical qualities of the people. The famous novelist wrote that in these flatlands *'God missed out the stairs'!*

Rectory in the Trees

CHRISTCHURCH

Malcolm D Allen

In the old days tragedy stalked the Fens. If it wasn't floods, the ugly face of rebellion defied the State and struck at the heart of the lower class, mainly those employed as fishermen and on the land.

Littleport has known tragedy born of an understandable cause and ending on the gallows. In 1816 feelings reached a peak and seething discontent burst into flames. Landworkers, together with soldiers returned from the Napoleonic wars who could find no work, attacked the homes of the wealthy and forced them to part with their money. Emboldened with success, the insurgents mounted punt guns on wagons and moved on to Ely to emblazon their grievances, holding the city to ransom. The military were called in and the rebels were crushed. Seventy were imprisoned and others put on ships en-route to Botany Bay. The five ringleaders were hanged at Ely and their bodies buried together in St. Mary's churchyard. No-one would lend a cart to convey the condemned men to the gallows, so the Bishop of Ely, chief magistrate, paid five guineas to provide one.

It is said that Littleport was founded by King Canute. It witnessed uprisings when the Fens were being drained and the livelihoods of workers and fishermen threatened. Shortages of food constantly inflamed the situation. The lofty tower of Littleport's ancient church witnessed these upheavals. The edifice has a rare feature, a double nave, and a wealth of beautiful, unusual stained glass windows including St. Crispin cobbling shoes and his brother Crispinian serving a customer.

Very serious floods occurred near Littleport, particularly in the late 1940s and early 1950s. Local men, helped by former German and Italian prisoners of war, prepared thousands of sandbags in an attempt to plug breached embankments along the River Great Ouse and, in other areas of the Fens, army vehicles were used to block gaps.

Railway lines were flooded and several homes and farms inundated by as much as seven feet. The floods caused a worrying delay in crop production and, at very considerable expense, emergency measures were taken to prevent the reoccurrence of the floods, including the cutting of a relief river.

The Great Ouse

AT LITTLEPORT

Mention ice skating and the locals will say "Made in the Fens!" When the washland is flooded a few days of hard frost transforms the water into glinting sheets of ice stretching for miles. When winter obliges – as it did in 2009-10 – local skaters and others from farther afield don rusting skates and enjoy themselves on vast reaches of frozen fen.

Skating takes place near Littleport and at Whittlesey Wash where part is kept flooded just in case. Important skating matches have taken place in the Fens, the first in 1763. Traditional long fen skates are very different from the short, modern kind. They were generally used for travelling from one place to another. The first skates were sharpened bones and these developed into iron skates made by local blacksmiths. Skates were used by Fen stilt walkers, their gait in the marsh compared with that of camels. The skates they used were called 'schaats' invented at the time of the drainage of the Fens in the 17th century.

Pleasure skating took place in the Fens in early times and eventually developed into serious competitive sport. The schaat was used for speed skating and Fenmen built up a deserved reputation for expertise on ice. They achieved astonishing speeds, bending their bodies forwards, hands linked behind them. When really speeding, skaters flail both arms in rhythmic, graceful motion. A beautiful sight.

Famous names emerged from the Fens and were spoken of far and wide, even in foreign lands. Names like 'Turkey' Smart and 'Fish' Smart were mentioned reverentially in public houses. Other famous Fen skaters had fascinating names such as 'Gutterpercha' See, 'Swearing Jack' Cooper and 'Chaffer' Legge among others. Give them a pair of 'schaats' and see them go!

John Guttan, who practiced on the frozen river at Nordelph, set up a record in 1821. A two-mile course was marked out and Guttan, blades biting the ice at more than 40 miles per hour, broke the tape in a remarkable two minutes and fifty-three seconds!

Fen skaters were tough men, physically honed to perfection usually working on farms lifting heavy bales of straw, following ploughs and digging out dykes. When they competed in international matches at home or abroad it was expected of them to bring back deservedly won trophies. And they did! The Fens were and still are, Jack Frost permitting, an ice skater's paradise.

A Skater's Paradise

LITTLEPORT

Fenland is still a watery place. Gone are the meres, taken over by numerous rivers, drains and dykes collecting water controlled by a sophisticated drainage system and fed into the outfalls.

Two such rivers of paramount importance are the Old and New Bedford rivers, the latter cut in 1650-1 to improve drainage of a vast area between Earith and Denver. Between these rivers extensive wash land is allowed to flood over in times of excessive rainfall to ease pressure on the embankments. The New Bedford river was cut at a sad price. That price was men's lives. After the Battles of Worcester and Dunbar (Scotland) during the Civil War, hundreds of Scottish and Dutch prisoners-of-war were brought to the Fens and set to work cutting rivers, including the New Bedford.

Several hundred Dutch sailors taken prisoner at a major sea battle off Portland Bill, Dorset, commenced work on the New Bedford river at Earith. It has a length of 21 miles and, like most of the Fens artificial waterways, it is as straight as an arrow. Scottish prisoners began work near Denver, Norfolk, with the two groups eventually meeting about halfway. An incredible feat but a sad one, as numerous prisoners susceptible to the moisture-laden environment and debilitating circumstances suffered from bronchial maladies and other related illnesses. Many died and the local people would not have them taken to burial grounds in the villages. Bodies were buried near or in the embankments the prisoners themselves had worked on.

Drainage commissioners looked after the prisoners as best as they could, but money for the scheme was in short supply and transport could not be provided. When we look over the vast reaches of fen, particularly the embanked rivers, we are looking at burial sites of more than 350 years ago.

Major drains were first given names but now they are called for instance, the Twenty Foot, the Forty Foot, the Sixteen Foot, the Hundred Foot – original widths. Most major drains are navigable and pleasure craft cruise along a myriad of natural rivers and artificial drains – a quiet, restful experience enriched by the unique canopy of variable three-quarter sky.

Drainage on the Fens

OLD BEDFORD RIVER

Malcolm D Allen

Seemingly far from the world's ignoble strife, the small city of Ely is the crown of the Cambridgeshire Fens and its cathedral, the jewel. In the past a defiant if political refuge it was the last place in England to hold William the Conqueror at bay. To set foot in this famous city is to be stirred with intellectual and spiritual enrichment of the grandeur of our heritage.

A lot has happened in Ely and many of its bishops were renowned, not merely for intellectual powers, but also for practical abilities. Bishop John Morton loved a challenge and he embraced the prospect of draining a large tract of fen between Guyhirn and Stanground. He built a tower at Guyhirn from which he could supervise work on the leam named after him. Morton's active brain dwelt on further improvements to the Fens but was thwarted by the War of the Roses. It was said of his dynamism that he passed away *'his head full of powers'*.

Then there is Oliver Cromwell, through and through a Fenman. Founder of the Commonwealth, Lord Protector Cromwell, self-styled Lord of the Fens, trained the initial elements of his redoubtable New Model Army, much emulated today, enlisting men from the Fens *'with the fear of God in them'*. At first against the drainage scheme, Cromwell later relented and became a strong advocate of it.

Another Fenman used Ely to great advantage. Everyone has heard of the epic resistance by Hereward the Wake against William the Conqueror. Ely served as his headquarters and even the monks took up arms against the invader. There is so much history of national importance associated with Ely, for instance the King's School famous for educational excellence. More than a thousand years old, it has the honour of having educated Edward the Confessor and cherishes links with the King's School at Westminster.

Lastly, we should not forget the architectural genius of Alan de Walsingham, a monk at Ely in the early 14th century who made light of a disaster when the cathedral's central tower collapsed. Walsingham envisaged the gaping hole over the rubble as a gateway to heaven and filled it with the uniquely famous octagon tower, the jewel of the Fens.

View from the Soham Road

ELY

The first thing visitors to Ely see is the magnificent Norman cathedral known as the Ship of the Fens. Next, they might care to stroll round the ancient precincts said to be the largest group of medieval buildings in Europe. Prior Crauden's chapel is worth a visit.

Ely may be a small city but it certainly isn't short of attractions. At the bottom of the hill flows the River Great Ouse on its way to the Wash. The river comes to life in spring and summer, moorings lined with numerous pleasure craft. Overlooking the Great Ouse, the shapely old Cutter Inn keeps watch over a truly idyllic scene. The inn is very popular with visitors entering Ely by road, rail and river, which is linked with the River Cam, Cambridge and St. Ives.

Ely Museum is worthy of a visit. Be prepared to be welcomed by a prostrate Roman skeleton discovered at Stuntney. The building was once a prison and some of the rooms are set out to resemble the bad old days a couple of hundred years ago.

Opposite the cathedral stands a large, handsome red-brick building formerly the Bishop's Palace. The large cannon situated on the Palace Green barked in anger during the Crimean War, but is now resigned to providing a background for people posing for photographs.

It is written that long ago, in the 11th century, King Canute often visited Ely by river and would order the rowers to stop so that he could listen to the monks chanting from the monastery overlooking the ancient city.

CRIMEAN CANNON, ELY

The Cutter and the

River Great Ouse

ELY

Cromwell received estates at Ely through the bequest of his uncle, Sir Thomas Stewart who died in 1636. He and his mother and family took up residence at Ely's charming old Glebe House which stands at the end of the city's picturesque green, and serves now as the Tourism Centre. It was here that Cromwell succeeded to the office of Farmer of the Tithes.

Living at Ely, Cromwell seized the opportunity of taking a keen, hard look at the coarse, industrious fen people and he liked what he saw. In later years an opponent wrote of Cromwell's regard for the Isle of Ely and its inhabitants:

> *'Colonel Cromwell told me he would make the Isle of Ely the strongest place in the world, and he would place in it a godly and precious people, and he would make it a place fit for God to dwell in.'*

The Isle of Ely became a strong place right enough. The pulpits were occupied by Ironsides preaching vigorously to congregations. The clergy listened in silence and conducted services in private homes. A strict Puritan was a dark clad miserable person who could not even bear the sight of a laughing child or people enjoying themselves. Not so with Cromwell. A deeply religious man he showed his true colours in his strong disapproval of ceremonial dogma and favoured simplicity of belief in accordance with Puritan principles. He was not, however, a miserable person; he had a sense of humour and attended races.

Nearby is St. Mary's Church, where five men, hanged for their part in the Littleport riots, are buried. They protested for fairer wages and better conditions and the gallows was their reward.

The view from Ely Cathedral's west porch towards Oliver Cromwell's house is a pleasant one. More than four centuries ago a far from pleasant event took place on the Green however. It was the scene of the burning at the stake of two men from Wisbech and Upwell respectively.

They died for refusing to recant over religious differences. The executioner placed oiled faggots around them and cast a sheet filled with New Testaments on the fire. Both men seized a copy and, clutching them to their chests, requested the onlookers to say Amen. It was written the men received the fire 'gratefully.'

Cromwell's House

ELY

Malcolm D.Allen

When excessive rain falls upon upland regions, low-lying rivers in the Fens swell, sometimes putting immense pressure on embankments. Water is allowed to spill onto 350-year old washland between the Bedford rivers and at Whittlesey Wash and Cowbit Wash. This prevents flooding of valuable agricultural land. When the water recedes washland reverts to fine grazing for sheep and cattle that grow fat as a result of 'good' flooding.

In the Fens it has not always been like that. Floods are synonymous with the serious inundations of 1947 and the 1950s. These were exceptional, and drastic measures were taken to bolster defences. A new relief river cut parallel to the River Great Ouse eliminated much of the risk of flooding in the eastern Fen region.

I remember redundant army vehicles being lowered into the breached bank of a Fen river to plug the gap. Anciently stakes were driven into the water's edge. If the stakes were suddenly exposed, observers knew that the bank had been breached somewhere along its length, and runners were dispatched to warn people to evacuate.

In living memory, 'bad' floods occurred at the time when harvest was ripe to bring in. Land workers had to row boats across the flooded fields to rescue sodden wheat sheaves, and flooded roads were greatly inconvenient to inhabitants.

In medieval times it was highly dangerous for individuals to venture too far across the marsh in winter when it became overlaid with water. Soft mud became a quagmire and sucked boats and occupants down. Mummified bodies were discovered when, centuries later, farmers turned the soil using deep ploughing techniques.

This exemplifies the challenge of the Fens; inhabitants losing ground to encroaching water and spending years reclaiming it. In modern times, advanced technology awaits the urgent hour. Sluices, embankments and numerous pumping units (one in the Middle Level, capable of discharging in excess of six million tons of water in a continuous pumping period of 24 hours) control the flow of water, thus ensuring that the historic and vital Fens continue to provide vast quantities of food for the nation.

Flooded Washes

IN THE FENS

At Wicken we tread in the footsteps of a famous family that changed the course of British history. To the little medieval church the Cromwells trudged sadly to bury their dead. Beneath a floor stone lies Henry Cromwell and beneath another slab was lowered in 1672 the mortal remains of Oliver Cromwell's sister, Elizabeth. In 1685 the memorial to the young Oliver Cromwell, one of the Lord Protector's grandsons, was placed here. The memorials are the main feature of the church and the chancel screen was given in the 20th century in memory of Henry Cromwell and his wife.

Henry Cromwell was, in Carlyle's words, *'a really honourable figure'*. He served in the Civil War under his famous father and became a colonel in charge of reinforcements in Ireland. He put forward several suggestions to help Ireland and said the army was playing too big a role in running that country. Henry, chief of the army in Ireland, ventured his views to the Council suggesting that Ireland should have a more constitutional government, but Parliamentary generals opposed him, saying the army should be in control.

Henry often threatened to resign but his father supervised his appointment as Lord Deputy of Ireland. Henry was very popular with the people and declined land worth £1,500 per year, saying that he could not receive it *'because Ireland was poor.'*

He settled in retirement at Wicken and farmed contentedly. Charles II, passing this way from Newmarket, decided to call upon Henry and an officer seized a pitchfork and carried it in mockery before farmer Cromwell.

Near the Wicken Fen Visitors' Centre stands a windmill rising proudly above the sedge. It was rescued from elsewhere and is the only survivor of hundreds in the Fens. A typical restored cottage is preserved in the approach lane to the Wicken Fen. Materials – sedge and willow and dried turf blocks taken from the Fen – match those used years ago, when cottages had to be flexible to equal shrinkage and expansion of marshy ground and it was necessary to build on pliable foundations.

The Wind Pump

WICKEN

Malcolm D Allen

An unspoilt lane leads from the village centre to Wicken Sedge Fen. Cared for by the National Trust, the Fen is a conservation area of great merit; internationally recognised and the habitat of numerous species of insects, wildlife and fauna. From 1899 it gradually increased and now covers about 900 acres or 360 hectares. It is planned to expand the wetland considerably in future. Wicken Fen was Britain's first nature reserve.

It is a magnificent sanctuary for wild birds such as mute swans, marsh harrier, cormorants, widgeon, snipe and reed warblers. There are many things to look out for; the common lizard loves basking in the sun or spot the harmless grass snakes slithering about their business. Water lilies galore adorn the lodes. Varieties of butterflies and damselflies flit above the sedge and plant life excels; guilder rose, marsh pea, milk parsley and so much more.

The Fen is superbly managed and volunteers do valuable work maintaining carr and woodland, cutting sedge, etc. During the Second World War part of the Fen was converted for agricultural use and, in the process, massive rock-hard bog oaks were extracted from beneath the surface where they had lain for hundreds of years. After the war, fields reverted to wet fen.

Wicken Fen offers lovely long and short walks along tracks hundreds of years old; the best are beside sedge-lined lodes, with the mere of particular interest. Boards are laid down for visitors to walk on, but bear in mind, although little water will be seen except in the mere, ponds and lodes, in places the ground is squelchy and stout boots or wellingtons are advisable.

After an enjoyable walk along tracks in the Fen observing the greenery and sedge, and relishing the quietness and stillness of nature at her very best, light refreshments can be bought near the reception. Here can be obtained a wealth of information about Wicken Fen including books about Fen life in general. The car park is spacious and toilets are nearby.

Sedge Fen

WICKEN

Malcolm D Allen

The first thing that struck me about Stretham was the old Georgian rectory used now as a place for autistic children. It is attached to a much older building, possibly a priest's home, dating back hundreds of years. Several years ago I was told by the rector that his children slept in other rooms away from the old house and the family dog never ventured along the passage leading to the medieval building. What lay beyond the door? Suffice to say I was informed that the appropriate authority decided the ancient building must not be disturbed or entered!

Stretham's fine old church stands near the old Roman road and incorporates parts of a Saxon and Norman edifice. The mortal remains of Nicholas de Kyngstone, a rector here nearly 700 years ago, had a fine brass of him but it was stolen. Joan Swan's brass is still intact, depicting her as a big woman who was surely proud of her two sons, both rectors at Stretham. Their mother died in 1497.

Outside the church, a stone cross erected in the 15th century probably marks the site of the medieval market place overlooking Akeman Street (A10). It escaped mutilation in the 16th century, the time of the Reformation. Stretham's lovely old windmill vies with the church tower for prominence and is visible from Ely, six miles away.

Along a narrow road leading to the Old West River stands a curious early 19th century pump house. Inside is a remarkable old beam engine, the derelict boilers housed in an attached building.

From the gantry above the engine visitors can view the massive iron beam turning the water wheel. It last worked in 1947. The machine is well looked after and can be turned for visitors by an electric motor showing the precise movements, but minus the hissing and spouting of steam!

The engine powered the 30 ft water wheel which was capable of lifting 30 tons of water in a single revolution. Several of these grand old engines were strategically situated in the Fens, earning the accolade, *'Thus water is by itself destroyed'*. They were eventually replaced by diesel powered pumps.

The Pump House

Stretham

Sutton's noble church tower unusually surmounted with an eye-catching double octagon is, in the writer's opinion, incongruously known as The Pepperpot. St. Andrew's is a large edifice perfectly matching the tower in sheer grandeur sitting on a high rise of land and clearly visible for miles across the flat Fens. Scottish prisoners-of-war cutting the New Bedford River in 1651 must have noticed the commanding sentinel and church which is dedicated to their own national saint.

The church was conceived by two of Ely's bishops towards the close of the 14th century. Bishop Arundel who crowned Henry IV and who possessed a trained eye for majestic ecclesiastical architecture, then reaching its peak, allied his vision to that of Bishop Barnet. In honour of these two men's expertise so grandly evidenced at Sutton, their arms and a portrait of Bishop Barnet appear in the upper porch room. This impressive example of church building at its expressive best is worthy of ranking architecturally with the country's small cathedrals.

The high ridge on which the 'Southern Farm' stands, affords marvellous views of the southern Fens, a myriad of colour in spring and summer, little lanes dropping down the slopes into what was once a watery wilderness. Prolific crops grew here in centuries past and added wealth to the village which became known as

Sutton Church Gate

'Golden Sutton'. Sutton escaped flooding but in the low depression south of the parish, an area parallel with the New Bedford river, Sutton Gault was disastrously inundated when rising water caused the river bank to collapse.

In 1774 Sutton received a visit from a great preacher and instigator of Methodism, John Wesley. The authorities would not, of course, allow him to speak in the church, so he happily verbalised in a commodious barn to a large congregation; a typical beginning in the advent of Methodism. A two-storey chapel, the idea of the Prior of Ely, and known as the Burystead Farm, was built at Sutton in the 14th century. Numerous burials took place on the site.

St. Andrew's Church

Sutton-in-the-isle

Along street and an assortment of Georgian houses and endearing cottages make Chatteris a typical Fen town. It was made famous in the 20th century as a place inextricably linked with a nationally famous Fen crop, carrots. Linked with the town is the well-known agricultural name, Arthur Rickwood, dubbed the Carrot King. Despite many changes since his time, the crop is still cultivated in the vicinity today.

Chatteris existed before the Norman Conquest and the town once had an abbey founded in the 10th century. All that survived was the Elizabethan manor house. Rubble and squared stone can be seen in garden walls of houses built on the former precincts of the religious community. The destitute nuns got into trouble for allowing animals to enter the abbey church and they eked out an existence from taking in lodgers.

A few bones of extinct animals were found at Chatteris by farmers and one ploughing a field turned up an urn containing a thousand Roman coins. The skeleton of an elephant owned by a travelling circus was discovered in more recent times. Vermuyden's Drain – the Forty Foot – nearby recalls the draining of the Fens by the great Dutch engineer of that name in Oliver Cromwell's century. Honey Farm near Chatteris honours the memory of St. Huna, steward to St. Etheldreda of Ely, who retired as a hermit to Chatteris in the 7th century.

Thanks to the generosity of a sexton's son who amassed a huge fortune in America, the commodious church was practically re-built in the early 20th century, but the 14th century tower and pillars testify to the older building which witnessed a devastating fire more than 600 years ago, almost wiping out the town. This was followed by another disastrous fire in more modern times which burnt down cottages in two of the streets.

158 men of Chatteris died in the First World War, among them George William Clare, V.C. a former chorister at the church. During a ferocious battle he carried a wounded comrade through intense fire and dressed the wounds of others brought to the post, then, realising the enemy was using gas, he risked death under fire and warned every post of the danger. At all times he was under fire by shot and shell. Finally he was killed. It is fitting that a Chatteris street is named after him.

Sunset over Chatteris

CHATTERIS

Malcolm D Allen

Charles I had a royal eye on Manea. He planned to acquire thousands of acres of marsh here knowing the drainage of the Fens, then a wonder of the world, would result in ultra-rich soil worth a king's ransom.

It was the King's intention to develop a magnificent estate at Manea with a fine palace and he would call it Charlemont – a sanctuary from the pressures of life in London. Before all this could take place Fenman Oliver Cromwell came onto the scene and the monarch lost his head, literally.

Manea, as in Mainee – some incorrectly pronounce it Main-ee-a – meaning 'island held in common', became the site of a social experiment. The famous socialist Robert Owen in 1838 dreamed up an 80 hectares co-operative within the parish, which is virtually a cul-de-sac divided by the Bedford rivers.

The community worked to their motto 'Each For All'. Everything started off well, the colonists building their own houses and working on the land. They were paid in vouchers exchanged at the co-operative store. They even organised recreation facilities and provided education for children and adults. The experiment failed through lack of finance and, more importantly, poor drainage. Rich Manea became poor Manea through repeated flooding.

The floods were brought on through numerous wind drainage engines passing water to each other and finally discharging it against Manea. Hundreds of these privately owned engines existed in the Fens and, although they did much good, they also did much harm, until the three Drainage Level Commissioners came into being with the latest technology and controlled the water more efficiently.

In the 1800s two land workers inspecting a newly drained field in the parish spotted two posts protruding from the mud. Their master told them to go back later and they found the posts were a wooden horse's tail and head set several feet apart. These were attached to a Danish longboat that had sunk more than a thousand years ago. The farmer ordered the men to chop the boat for kindling and placed the head above the entrance to his house. Thus Manea lost the opportunity to become the Fens' very own Sutton-Hoo.

The Warden's Bicycle

MANEA

Whenever I mention March, I sense the evocative aroma of steam and grease tinged with a hint of coal smoke. After the Second World War March's vast Whitemoor railway complex was the largest working marshalling yard in Europe. More than 200 steam locos of various classifications were based at March and the sprawling yards held up to 17,000 wagons and trucks. Whitemoor was a rail buff's paradise. The railway at March was rejuvenated in recent years and supplies ballast to all parts of the country.

Smoky March, as it was once known, has seen a few famous faces. Martin Pierson, a composer of music, lived here a few centuries ago and had the pleasure of hearing his music played before royalty. John Wilson claimed to be the world's most famous pedestrian. He walked through many countries and, mistaken for a spy, was threatened with shooting and almost ended up in a cannibal tribe's cauldron!

One of March's most acclaimed sons, William 'Billy' Barker, worked in the early 1800s as a bargee on the town's river. On the advent of the railway, river trade diminished and Billy became redundant. This prompted him to go to London to find work. Jobs were hard come by in the 1850s and Billy joined thousands of other workless men in the gold rush to California. Disappointed at negative results he moved to Canada and prospected there.

When his colleagues moved on, Billy sank a deep shaft in Williams Creek and brought to the surface 1,000 kilograms of gold. It made him a fortune of 500,000 dollars – a massive amount at the time. He was regarded as a generous and helpful man. His hard won wealth eventually ran out and, like his parents at March, Billy died a pauper.

Barkerville is named after him, as is a mountain and a river. A festival held each year honours the March man who, it might be said, founded British Columbia. Billy Barker is very much part of modern Canada's school curriculum.

Railway Ghosts

MARCH

Malcolm D. Allen

Pleasantly situated on the River Nene (old course), March treasures its fine old church, formerly a pilgrimage chapel, extravagantly adorned with an internationally famous medieval roof displaying 118 oak angels, each in the pose of flying. Said by experts to be the finest of its kind, the roof was made by 16th century Suffolk craftsmen and brought to March in about 1525. It honours the Creator and his handmaiden, St. Wendreda who died at March in the late 7th century. Her relic was enshrined in the church building refashioned in the 14th century as a pilgrimage chapel, and she is credited with the posthumous conversion of Canute, the pagan who later became a good King of England. Novelist Dorothy Sayers' parents lived at nearby Christchurch, and Dorothy was known to have visited the church.

Situated not far from March, and sharing the second largest 'island' in the Cambridgeshire Fens, is Wimblington which boasts a large Victorian edifice of a church with a massive tower. Like a good many other churches it experienced hard times. Pleasingly, it serves a multi-purpose role in village social life, offering a library and other useful areas apart from the usual services. It might be likened to medieval churches that opened their doors to meetings and even found space to store grain in times of abundance.

Wimblington also has a few old houses of note, the oldest dating back to the 17th century. Georgian influence springs to the eye in the midst of modern estates developing towards March.

These fine houses were built by gentlemen farmers with foresight of the great potential wrested from the marsh. The undrained Fens served islanders well in their pursuit of wild-fowl and management of numerous fisheries and reed beds. Eels were taken in tens of thousands and used in payment to the Lord of the Manor, in this case the Bishop of Ely. Eels were a rich source of supply to upland regions and highly sustainable to the Fen economy. The prelate had a palace at Doddington and his influence, not always welcome, affected Wimblington in more ways than one.

St. Wendreda's Church

MARCH

Malcolm D'Allen

Visitors to March remark that the town strongly resembles a Thames-side village. This is understandable; the old course of the River Nene passing beneath the bridge meanders between banks flanked by open grass areas and riverside gardens creating a splendid vista beneath leafy canopies which go on and on. The scene is very un-Fenlike.

There is a truly memorable welcome to water-people in spring and early summer when nature's colours are at their best. They come in narrow boats and cruisers from places as far away as Bedford and Leeds. Many like to moor at the wharfs to stock up and stay for a night or two. It could not be easier for visitors; the moorings are conveniently situated each side of the bridge in the town centre.

The riverside walks are very pleasant, West End in particular, where a number of old cottages and houses can be seen, some dating back to the 1600s. Owners keep the river bank neat and prim and gardens are much to be admired. On the opposite side of the river, the large central park is very popular with visitors and townspeople alike. It adjoins the modern library and covered-in swimming pool.

A stone's throw away, overlooked by Britannia surmounting the impressive tower, the town hall of continental design lords it over the market place which was opened in 1671. The market was moved to its present place near the river from an older site to centralise it between the ancient communities of Merche and Mercheford merging together in the 13th century. The market drew its strength from the river trade and it still proves very convenient to river tourists.

Anciently, the river gave access to Whittlesey Mere, southern England's largest fresh water lake and the scene of numerous regattas in the 18th century.

An ardent diarist, Lord Orford, commander of several residential barges passing through March to the Mere in the 18th century was not a bit complimentary to March women, the Admiral of the Fleet writing that they were the ugliest he had ever seen. In those days life was hard and debilitating in the Fens. The women were tough and muscular; they had to be. But the writer happily testifies that nowadays March ladies are dainty, elegant and pretty. It's amazing what a few hundred years of progress will do. Put that in your pipe and smoke it, my lord.

Riverside

MARCH

Malcolm D Allen

Whittlesey is a pleasant market town situated a few miles from Peterborough. The market place with its ancient buttercross is flanked by an assortment of interesting old buildings, some in the process of being restored. The beautiful tower of St. Mary's church, topped with the finest spire in Cambridgeshire, peeps over the roofs. A stone's throw away the medieval church of St. Andrew shows off its imposing exterior.

Whittlesey's famous son, General Wakelyn Smith, sleeps in the local cemetery, and a bust in St. Mary's honours the man who fought at Waterloo and became Governor of the Cape in 1847. Ladysmith, a town in South Africa, honours the general's wife. Another Whittlesey worthy, William Whittlesey, became Archbishop of Canterbury in 1368. He protested against the heavy taxation of the clergy from the pulpit of old St. Paul's and collapsed. Taken to Lambeth Palace by boat, he later died.

Whittlesey is famous for production of domestic bricks and, at one time, 40 kiln chimneys belched smoke much to the chagrin of housewives. Only five remain now. Clay pits have yielded fossilised remains of prehistoric beasts.

The former mere south of the town was England's largest fresh water lake and had a circumference of 12 miles. Many regattas were held on its bright blue waters, and it was much favoured by Lord Orford, admiral of a fleet of barges navigating the old course of the Nene.

The Mere was drained in 1851 by the world's first centrifugal pump built by Appold and exhibited at the Great Exhibition. It pumped 1,680 gallons per minute. In the process a prehistoric oak dug-out canoe, a wild boar's skull and that of a wolf, and a censer from Ramsey abbey came to light. Most amazing of all the skeleton of a killer whale caused minds to wonder. The land transformed from Whittlesey Mere shrank considerably and where a wealth of wildlife could be found, vast acreages of gently waving crops of wheat abound.

Whittlesey at work

WHITTLESEY

Malcolm Dillon

The village of Thorney began as a holy place, Ancarig meaning island of anchorites, who chose to live here in 670. A great abbey developed and part of it remains, in the sombre Norman style, looking across to an expanse of green complemented by fine houses built of blocks of stone from the abbey. It is now the parish church and exudes simplicity and strength and we can only imagine how it looked when it was five times as large.

Visitors to Thorney may find themselves in a dilemma. They are caught in a time warp set in the Victorian age, grand-looking stone clad buildings belying the fact that Thorney really is in the Fens and not in the Cotswolds. Ducal influence is everywhere. Here you find bowers of greenery in the lanes and gabled houses look across fine vistas. Rows of uniform estate houses testify to the munificence of the Duke of Bedford who, in the mid 1800s, transformed Thorney into a veritable paradise.

Unlike many of his ilk the Duke envisaged Thorney as the ideal place to evolve a management system never before witnessed in Britain. Sheer magnificence can be seen in estate buildings built in the pseudo-Jacobean style with Victorian practicality. The ordering of it brought fame and recognition to this part of the Fens.

Radical development was largely experimental and it amply benefited the owner and his workforce. His efficacy was outstanding and he gave the community a water-filtration plant, decent housing, a fire station, gas works and allotments as well as a library, community centre and a school.

The system practiced at Thorney *was the most successful experiment in social organisation that England has so far seen*. It has been professionally acknowledged that there is no village in England with a more extensive display of well designed Victorian cottage architecture than that at Thorney.

The Duke wrote that the inhabitants have their reward in the health of Thorney, in the practical disappearance of crime and the extinction of pauperism. In 1912 taxation and bad seasons brought the grand experiment to an untimely end.

Fish and Chips

THORNEY

Hong Lok Garden 永利園 Fish and Chips

Malcolm D Allen

Centuries ago, anyone travelling in the vicinity of Whittlesey and Thorney during the summer would see crops of lustrous green. This was an inedible plant of the cabbage family called colza, valued for its oily content to soften wool and used in lamps. Divided by wheat crops, it presented a pretty patchwork in the fields.

Huguenot colonies were set up at Whittlesey and Thorney, the latter becoming the centre of activities, with Huguenots and Walloons receiving permission to worship at the abbey church in the French tongue. Incidentally, several old houses near Thorney are built of squared stone said to have been obtained when the Norman abbey was dissolved. The stone made very substantial buildings for farmers and one, at least, built his house in the French style. It is known to have been occupied years ago by a French family.

The Huguenots and their French-speaking Walloon counterparts were skilled in land drainage techniques and hired or purchased land in the area, cultivating it and producing excellent crops. The colony at Thorney numbered a few hundred souls; most families chose to live in the countryside and generally kept themselves to themselves, working industriously and practising continental traditions.

One of the colony's practices was that of paring the land using the French paring plough to raise wheat stubble, then make it into heaps and set light to it. The ashes were scattered over the land and ploughed in. In more recent times stubble in fields was set alight before the plough was used. After harvest this became a regular practice and spread all over the Fens and beyond. Stubble burning created a lot of smoke and could wreath roads in a dangerous obnoxious mist.

Nowadays burning stubble and making bonfires is illegal. In early times and, until fairly recently, stubble burning caused fires to creep beneath the surface and peat to smoulder. Fire brigades were called out to extinguish them.

Stubble Burning

BURNING THE EARTH

Parson Drove is a very long village with two churches, one built in the Victorian era, the other – St. John the Baptist – dating to the 13th century and almost entirely made new two hundred years later after a devastating flood. The chancel was never rebuilt. Centuries ago Parson Drove was an outpost in the bleak Fens and clergy from Leverington travelled along the Drove to hold services in St. John's church, now sadly redundant. Three hundred years ago the church was used by a colony of Huguenots and Walloons led by their minister Rev. Pujolas. They were all refugees from religious persecution and some of their descendants can still be found in the Fens. Hardly any English people attended the services which were held in the French tongue!

Woad crops were harvested from the fertile fields of the parish and a unique woad mill existed here producing blue dye for staining garments using the same process as did ancient Brits to scare the Romans. Woad was crushed to pulp by a wheel turned by horses and moulded into balls, then stacked into a shed to dry. After a considerable time they were drenched in water and left to ferment in a darkened chamber for several weeks. The balls were then ready to distribute to manufacturers of cloth garments. The practice ceased when modern manufacturing methods took over and the woad mill, the only one in the country, became derelict.

Famous diarist Samuel Pepys spent a day or two visiting his aunt at The Swan Inn. He was not impressed and complained that his room was cold and the bed damp. To make things worse his horse was stolen and he testily penned that Parson Drove was a *'heathen place'*. He commented that his journeys in the Fens were plagued by the region's dreaded stinging gnats. Near The Swan, the village lock-up, built in 1829, overlooks a pleasant green. It was later used to house the fire engine.

John Peck, a very prominent farmer, lived at the village in the 19th century. He kept a daily diary of events and noted the hard times affecting farmers and population. The diary mentions high costs of food and poor returns for farmers. This hasn't just happened in our own times! Mr. Peck was instrumental in making the New North Level Main Drain and the sluice at Clough's Cross.

The Swan Inn

PARSON DROVE

Breadbasket of the nation: this is no idle boast. For more than 150 years, the Fens have produced ever increasing tonnages of crops for the national larder. Production reached its peak in the Second World War when Britain became reliant on home-grown food.

Since then technology has changed the course of things, improving management of peat and silt land and encouraging stronger prolific crops, inevitably adding to a reduction in replacement of manpower. Farmers engaged in specialised crop production rely increasingly on revolutionary machinery and land workers traditionally using hoes are seldom seen nowadays.

Traverse the Fens in appropriate seasons and real beauty greets the eyes; fields of potatoes bearing pale purple flowers overhang neatly mounded rows. This is in vivid contrast to fields of rape, a plant with bright yellow flowers used for oil and fodder. It is good as a preparatory crop too. Sugar beet grows profusely and is stacked by the side of roads for transporting to sugar factories

One hardy annual is wheat which is grown prodigiously on a patchwork quilt of fields anciently producing sedge. The crop has graced the Fens for 300 years and became extensive as more and more acres were drained. Damp wheat is a farming problem but nowadays large drying units are normal. Asparagus grows well and celery thrives on black land.

Chatteris carrots excel and were first grown as fodder for livestock. Onions, too, are produced in the Fens. Crops grown in the Fens are washed and pre-packed for shops and supermarkets all over the country.

Fruit crops are grown mainly on silt land and greensand but foreign competition tends to diminish output. However you still can't beat a good Fen apple. Pears, plums and, of course, strawberries are also prolific.

Potato fields

IN THE FENS

WORK IS DONE

If we were to ascend the west tower of Ely Cathedral, we would see in every direction a vast panorama of flat landscape, one of the most historic regions in Britain. It is England's Holland, covering 865 square miles wrested long ago from swamps and transformed by the prodigious efforts of men into ultra-rich soil. In Holland the emphasis is to keep the sea at bay. In the Cambridgeshire Fens the battle is waged against fresh water draining into the low-lying level, a natural sump, from surrounding upland counties.

North Cambridgeshire generally lies very low, in places beneath sea level. Near Cambridge it rises up to 450 feet – the so-called East Anglian Heights. There is a big comparison with the Heights of South Cambridgeshire and the Lows of Fenland.

Indomitable, determined spirit characterises true Fenmen of modern times as it did in days of yore. Bearing in mind state-of-the-art technology and know-how passed down along the ages, one might be a little rash in saying that the Fenmen's skill and patience has at last conquered Mother Nature.

Man's efforts introduced a different beauty to the Fens and, more importantly, the low land is highly profitable to cultivate. It did, and still does, provide food in abundance for the nation, a fact which earned it the title of the Nation's Larder.

Drained by a succession of eminent engineers, the land is preserved with great care. There are hardly any hedges, and few trees. Fields are separated by ditches and drains communicating with wider cuttings.

The Fens can change in the twinkling of an eye – cloaked by mist, caressed by warm sunlight, moistened by storms and showers, crops bending before the wind sometimes causing the dreaded 'Fen Blow' – fine dust where nature has been known to transfer seeds from fields into towns. A patchwork quilt of peaceful fields reflected in a myriad of waterways. And above all, the expansive overhead canopy of light and colour. This is the land of three quarter sky stretching from horizon to horizon just as it did when the Fens were similar to the American Everglades.

Nothing compares with sunrise and sunset bathing the Fens in translucent hues and indescribable brightness.

Fenland Reflections

THE FENS

Outlook over the Fens

A New Harvest

In its former state the Fens was regarded as a prolific, irregular expanse of marsh with an abundance of wildfowl and numerous fisheries supplying the needs of domestic tables in many regions of the country. The lowland harvest found a ready market in places as far away as London and Birmingham. Fenmen using flat-bottomed boats transported huge quantities of eels, fish, wildfowl and reeds to the Fen perimeters. Produce was loaded onto articulated vehicles of great length drawn by as many as half a dozen horses to areas in the south, midlands and the north of the country. The economy of the Fens was heavily based on natural produce and it is not surprising that Fenmen objected vigorously to plans to rid the lowland of water. They regarded this as a direct threat to their livelihood and were inspired to direct destructive forays on sluices, embankments and wind engines. The following verse captures the widespread temperament of the times:

> *'Come brethren of the water and let us all assemble*
> *To treat upon the matter which makes us quake*
> *and tremble,*
> *For we shall rue it, if 't be true that the Fens be*
> *undertaken,*
> *And when we feed in fen and reed,*
> *They'll feed both beef and bacon.'*

The vision of the drainage undertakers was shared by few inhabitants and how and when to bring the new harvest into effect proved indeterminable. From the 15th century most Fen towns such as Chatteris, Whittlesey, Littleport, Ely and March were classed as minor ports linked by a myriad of natural waterways. The towns had their own fleets of barges conveying a wide range of local goods to King's Lynn, Peterborough, Cambridge and Bedford and all places in between. The provision of new drains – the Forty Foot, Sixteen Foot, Twenty Foot, and the Old and New Bedford rivers which were linked to the River Ouse, the River Nene and the old circular course of the Nene – provided easy access to Fen parishes as well as those in the encompassing upland areas.

Materials carried by barges and fen wherries were varied and included coal, timber, stone and perishable items. Fen rivers were essential highways at a time when parishes were virtually isolated and roads did not exist. The rivers were vital to the Fens economy. As late as 1920 large amounts of water-borne goods were taken via rivers to Wisbech with its inland sea-port. There, produce and materials were transferred onto ships destined for the Baltic and several continental ports. Water-borne goods were destined for King's Lynn and Boston; wealthy towns enhanced by their membership to the Hanseatic League, a medieval form of Common Market without the politics.

From 1850, when most fields had been wrested from the marsh, fen barges and lighters worked the waterways on a regular basis and predominantly carried sugar beet, wheat and processed flour to a variety of destinations. From the end of the Second World War the rivers became relatively quiet and gradually tourists with their own or hired cruisers and narrowboats boosted tourism in the Fens where 300 miles of waterways became navigable. This is a much appreciated fillip to the Fens' economy.

In the early 19th century, transport along roads was hazardous, particularly in winter, with some roads better described as rutted earth tracks and quite impassable. It was not until the 20th century that most roads were given tarmac surfaces and increasing commercial traffic on the roads together with the inauguration of the railway brought about the demise of commercial traffic along the rivers. From the early 1800s minor roads began to appear and served a rapidly increasing number of farms occupying sites formerly covered by water. Country lanes giving access to farms and small communities were affected by winter weather and it became normal for urban councils to contract farmers to roll road surfaces in the spring.

Farmers living in safe havens on the uplands looked interestingly at the drainage work. Some, realising the potential the Fens had to offer, purchased large tracts of marsh and bided their time for land to dry out. In the late 17th century and 18th century fine houses were built by farmers in Fen towns and they lived in them confidently and expectantly before building farm houses on their estates.

Men made redundant in various parts of the country came in masses to the Fens to take up work on the land as farm workers. This resulted in a housing crisis and townspeople took the labourers in as lodgers and even built low, airless rooms onto existing properties. In the mid 1850s there was no such thing as planning permission and this led to a motley assortment of ramshackle, insanitary lodges conducive to serious outbreaks of cholera and typhoid fever arising from water supplies drawn from contaminated public and private wells. As in the American gold rush when thousands of men left Britain, it was inevitable that madams followed immigrants to the Fens.

A hundred years ago teams of women, pursuing a different career, and riding bone-shaker cycles were a familiar sight in the Fens. They would cycle miles along country roads generally in teams of eight or ten wearing bonnets to protect their heads from the sun and searing winds which swept the Fens, occasionally stirring up dust storms known as the Fen Blow. These hardy women thought nothing of pressing pedals fifteen miles a day to and from fields where, armed with hoes, they patiently took out weeds from between rows of beet. By 1900 a large acreage was devoted to potato, wheat and sugar beet and this led to considerable employment of local people. In wartime, when there was a serious shortage of food, Fen folk contributed magnificently to the nation's wellbeing. In modern times, main crops produced in the Fens are still wheat, potato and sugar beet which develop particularly well on peat soil, whereas the adjoining silt lands reclaimed from the sea are more suitable for brassica, fruit and the cultivation of tulips and roses.

The undrained fen produces its own water-loving plant life such as razor-sharp sword-edge reed which, if handled carelessly, will cut the hand to the bone. Reeds are the hallmark of the Fens and can be seen almost everywhere surviving in ditches and at the edge of ponds. The Fens' sword-edge reed is well known for its great durability and it is very popular for thatching purposes, even more so than Norfolk reed. Rape seed covering the land with a mass of yellow flowers is used extensively by farmers and is particularly good as an introductory crop on virgin land. It is also very popular in Holland on land reclaimed from the sea. The woad plant once thrived in the Fens and did particularly well on silt land. It was grown and processed for bluish dye and, until the early 20th century, it was harvested at Parson Drove and Spalding. Woad mills were worked by horses dragging the press, crushing woad in a circular motion.

Decoys could be seen here and there in the ancient Fens. These comprised ponds hidden by alders and reeds to attract wild fowl which were driven by barking dogs running along the bank frightening them into wire-covered channels where they were trapped and killed. Drainage had a destructive effect on fen plants and wild-fowl. In those times, Fenmen were called Fen sloggers and they were adept at walking on stilts on marshy ground. Fen sloggers used long wooden poles which they called poy sticks to assist them when leaping across narrow water courses and retrieving wild fowl.

In historic and modern terms the Fenland with its myriad of natural and artificial waterways, long ago a dreary waste of obnoxious decay covered with a permanent vapour, by man's ingenuity and stoical endeavour is now an artificial landscape of immense value to the nation. It broke men's backs and claimed lives to reward us with a profitable and immeasurable contribution to our own day and age. To call it a miracle is an understatement.

THE IRON HORSE BRINGS FAME TO THE FENS

The inauguration of the railways had a marked effect on the Fens. The iron horse contributed hugely to the Fenland economy with almost every village having a station with sidings set aside for use by farmers. Increasing convenience using rail facilities introduced a highly efficient mode of transportation vital to the Fens where crops could be transported to far-flung destinations.

In 1845 the Eastern Counties railway laid lines from Newport to Cambridge through Ely and, in 1846 to Brandon where it joined the Norfolk railway thus enabling the first through services between London and Norwich. Lines north to King's Lynn and north-west to March and Peterborough followed in 1847. The Ely, Sutton and St. Ives branch line opened in 1878. Running through the central area the Great Eastern Railway's Ely and Peterborough branch line had access to a most prolific agricultural area passing through several villages strategically important to the commercial interests of the Fens' agricultural community.

The first railway line to reach Wisbech, Cambridgeshire's inland port, opened in May 1847. The town had two stations, one a terminus on the South Brink. A year later this line was lengthened to connect with the East Anglian railway to Watlington (Magdalen Road) and the second station was built. These stations were used by the Eastern Counties and East Anglian railways until about 1851. From 1845-50 rival schemes for lines to Peterborough via Wisbech and Sutton Bridge came under scrutiny by the Great Northern and Eastern Counties railway companies. Wisbech Corporation objected to the building of another bridge over the River Nene as it would present a hazard to shipping. An alternative was proposed by the Eastern Counties railway company and the line laid down in 1866.

Each company laid down branch lines to the quays, the Midland and Great Northern terminating at the Old Market. In 1883 the Great Eastern Company opened a steam tram line from Wisbech to Outwell, extending it to Upwell in 1884. The line, featured in the Reverend Awdry's *Thomas the Tank Engine* series, was never economical although it continued in use until after the Second World War. Passenger services ended in 1927 but commercial goods and fruit were carried on the line until 1966. Dr Beeching's radical reform of the national railway system deprived Wisbech of its stations and the nearest station was that at March. The line from Wisbech to March still exists but is redundant at the time of writing. A private consortium calling itself the Bramley Line is hoping to restore this line to use, thus connecting Wisbech to March which has lines to Peterborough, Ely and Cambridge. The loss of its railway connections coupled with a downturn in local horticulture caused a lot of damage to Wisbech.

The railway came as an unexpected blessing to March. The town's status as the major rail centre in Cambridgeshire had a huge effect on the Isle of Ely's railway population. In 1921 a surprisingly high percentage (22.3%) of the working population of March was employed on the railway, proportionately three times as many as Swindon. The Isle of Ely as a whole had a greater proportion of people working on the railway with the exception of Cumberland and the Soke of Peterborough. By 1931 the concentration of rail workers in the Isle exceeded that of Cumberland. Percentages were: the Soke 9.2; the Isle of Ely 4.8; and Cumberland 3.6. March itself rated overwhelmingly at 24.5.

At the beginning of the 20th century March urban district contained 30 square miles of farmland in addition to the town, and farm workers almost equalled railwaymen. Railway workers were known locally as the 'elite' and earned far more than did the farming fraternity. One of the greatest benefits to March having the railway was that the town became accessible to all parts of Cambridgeshire and East Anglia.

Little did the Eastern Counties Railway board realise that the permanent way from Wisbech to Cambridge would prove for March such a beneficial omen, albeit to the frustration of Wisbech. With its port, Wisbech had great ambitions of harnessing the advantages of steam and sail. The Eastern Counties Railway board desired to consolidate its position and sought to construct a rail centre at Wisbech. The Peckover family, bankers and ardent Quakers, owned a considerable estate at Wisbech. Lord Peckover was approached by the railway company with the intention of purchasing sufficient land on which to develop the rail centre. Sensing the immense benefits this would have for the Borough, he agreed to selling the company land, but imposed an unacceptable condition to the effect that the railway company refrain from working on Sundays.

The Isle of Ely County Council and March Urban District Council were approached and agreed that the railway company acquire land at March for the development of the new yard. At first, the councils objected to the proposition but the fact that the town's population had decreased by 12 per cent won the day. The yard was built in 1883 near the railway station and this encouraged the Isle of Ely County Council, who had hired a so-called neutral hall at March for its meetings, to anchor roots conveniently near March station. The County Hall at March was built in 1908 much to the annoyance of the Wisbech burghers still smarting from losing the rail centre. Councillors from all over the county travelled to March and it became the County town.

Development of the railway yard and the County Hall caused March to expand rapidly in a northern direction. The old railway station was replaced by one a few hundred yards from the level crossing in order to prevent disruption from trains standing on the crossing. Other improvements took place west of the station and set the pace for further major developments in later years. For March, the 1880s was a decade of consolidation, foundations laid in readiness for what would be the most-up-to-date and largest railway marshalling yards in the country and, at the end of World War Two, the largest of its kind in Europe.

This dramatic augmentation was occasioned by exceptionally heavy delays in the original yard which had a domino effect as far as Peterborough. It led to a new Up yard being developed at Whitemoor, slightly north of March, which came into operation on March 3rd, 1929. The yard could accommodate 4,000 wagons and served 350 destinations. At that time Britain had little experience of bidirectional mechanical yards and the L.N.E.R approached German experts for advice and equipment. The company purchased hydraulic retarders (rail brakes) from Froehlich, a German engineering firm. This company also designed the lookout tower and equipped it with state-of-the-art electrically operated consoles for operating the gravitational hump and retarders. The tower and that on the Down yard were typically Teutonic in design and were very similar to lookout towers built at detention camps in Germany.

This yard was eminently successful and inspired provision of the new Down yard which ushered Whitemoor into full operation. On January 13th, 1933 the local newspaper printed a broad sheet page devoted to the new yards emblazoned with the headline 'March's Claim To World Fame'. It highlighted the opening of the new Down yard which cost £300,000. The new yards with gravitational marshalling techniques proved a huge enhancement to movement of traffic. On completion of the new Down yard 6,000 wagons could be held in reception. A mineral section with ten reception sidings accepted 926 wagons, and 40 marshalling sidings received 3,647 wagons. Four sidings held 200 crippled wagons. Astonishingly, both Up and Down yards at their peak could accommodate 17,273 wagons. The new extension brought the total cost of the complete system to £600,000, then an immense expenditure.

Following this major improvement many more engines were used and it became necessary to extensively enlarge the loco department (31B) enabling well over 200 steam locomotives to be housed and serviced. An idea as to the size of the March depot is gained by comparing it with the old depot at King's Cross terminus which accommodated 95 engines and was considered large. Other additions were preparation sheds and a power house with huge dynamos, two well-fitted mess rooms for staff and a large store room and offices, plus an engineers' room. The Down tranship shed was particularly busy and constantly in use. Miles of rail was laid over the new Down yard. The mammoth scheme to up-date Whitemoor provided employment for a great many conversant with all capacities of skills, and much of the labour was provided locally.

During the Second World War a decoy yard sited at Stags Holt, a couple of miles from Whitemoor, comprised oil drums and hundreds of lights which were placed in fields and lit up to attract the attention of enemy pilots flying solitary aircraft. When necessary a total blackout was imposed on the real yards. All this was supposed to mislead enemy airmen into thinking they were flying over the real thing. Surely even they, seeing the lights below, would think it to be a ruse. The enemy often bombed approaches to the yards, destroying rails and causing disruption, but it was conjectured that the Luftwaffe deliberately avoided mass destruction to preserve Whitemoor for their own use following the expected invasion. A hundred bomber raid could have easily destroyed the marshalling yards. As it was, Whitemoor took only one direct hit, but the dummy yard did have a few isolated enemy visitors early in the war.

With its potential benefits, the railway revolutionised every aspect of life in the country and Whitemoor contributed handsomely both on a national scale and locally. The iron horse drew an indelible line beneath the fortunes of the Fens and the marshalling yards with a force of more than 2,000 employees made an outstanding contribution to the national war effort. No-one could envisage the change that was to come. Steam power was coming to an end and diesel traction taking over. Short wheel base wagons were giving way to the long wheel base variety which rendered hump shunting obsolete. It was hard to believe that Whitemoor would shudder to a halt, but it did. Technological advancement and economic considerations put the brake on operations. Eventually the diesel department closed down and the vast yards fell eerily silent. In a short space of time they had deteriorated into a wasteland littered with the wrecks of burnt out cars.

A Phoenix Rises above the Fens

For many years Whitemoor remained the property of the railway company, until the Home Office visualised redundant Whitemoor as an ideal place to build a high grade prison and purchased part of the land contaminated by sulphur deposits and diesel oil. After the prison had been built, 43.7 hectares remained in limbo awaiting a solution. This came from the railway itself and the phoenix spread its wings.

Initially Network Rail inspected sixteen existing sites with their new Local Distribution Centre in mind. For various reasons, usually inadequate size, most fell short of the company's requirements. Whitemoor at March covered a large area and, despite being slightly out of the way, it offered a viable option. Following approval to develop the LDC by Cambridgeshire County Council, government approval followed in 2003. Thirty million pounds vitalised the development which includes space for a concrete sleeper plant and state-of-the-art recycling facilities.

With the exception of the 80-year-old listed water tower which has been restored, other buildings dating from the steam and diesel eras were pulled down. The tower overlooking the new centre provides water for the site including dust control in ballast stockpiles. During development of Phase One, thousands of tons of track covered the site, and buildings have been erected, long sidings provided and internal roads laid down making access possible. Nothing has been wasted, recycling very much an issue. Unwanted earth was used to create bunds to minimise noise against residential properties nearby. Another feature of this welcome new awakening at Whitemoor included conservation of wildlife – existing colonies of great crested newts for instance, with new ponds being created to replace old ones.

The LDC comprises twenty-six train stabling sidings, five wagon maintenance and fuelling facilities and four ballast loading and unloading sidings. Modern ballast wagons are equipped with diesel engines to power hopper doors. The new centre was provided with all-round state-of-the-art equipment. For 150 years March contributed immeasurably to the function of Britain's railway systems and, thanks to the development of Network Rail's new distribution centre, Whitemoor continues to be a famous name in a changing, yet increasingly vital, distribution network. For the town, it introduced the spirit of re-birth.

The Present and the Future

For hundreds of years the Fens have replenished the plates of the nation, be it provision of wildfowl, fish, bountiful crops, wheat and root, or fruit on a grand scale. This vital contribution to the country's larder is likely to continue, the region recognised by the government as being well worthy of preservation and that all means be taken to prevent the Fens from reverting to a watery waste.

The multi-million pound investment in the new pumping station at Wiggenhall St. Germans replacing the old worn out drainage units indicates the government's and Middle Level Commissioners' intention to protect the Fens from being inundated in seasons of extreme rain and snow.

Rising sea levels in future could be a threat and it is important that the sea embankments around the Wash are maintained in good repair. Some embankments date from the medieval era and even earlier and it is vital that the sea is held back. In the past the sea whipped to a frenzy by severe storms broke the barriers and water reclaimed thousands of acres of marsh being prepared for agricultural production. It also played havoc with the outfalls, silt building up and preventing rivers from discharging properly into the sea. It is important that the Fens' highly efficient drainage system be maintained to the highest standard. If the system were to fail the consequences would be disastrous to the upland regions as well as the highly productive lowland area, much of which is below sea level.

Most Fen rivers are navigable and emphasis is increasingly being placed on tourism. Every year thousands of visitors enter the Fens in private and hired narrow boats and cruisers. Many make use of marinas at Ely and March. Cars and coaches are becoming more numerous bringing tourists from all areas of the country to Ely, Wisbech, Peterborough and March. Special attractions exist, amongst which are the famous cathedrals at Ely and Peterborough and a host of renowned churches with acclaimed features such as the fine medieval tower at Sutton-in-the-Isle with its double octagon, and the octagons at Ely cathedral and at Upwell. Octagons are a notable feature in low countries. It is said that in medieval times lights shone from these towers to guide workers in the marsh to the safety of the islands. Bells, too, were rung when the Fens were overcome by swirling mist. Some Victorian churches, built away from the islands, have insecure foundations and certain towers and buildings have had to be demolished.

Other areas of the Fens are being deliberately allowed to revert to marsh to attract wildlife, flora and insects, and that is a good idea. To see the pre-drainage Fens at their best, I recommend Wicken Fen and just beyond the Cambridgeshire border, Welney Wildlife Centre and Wetland Trust eight miles from March where, in winter, thousands of geese and swans from Russia inhabit open water near the New Bedford river. There are several hides from which to observe the birds and photograph them. These wildlife centres are very popular and attract visitors from vast distances.

The Fens can best be described as the land of the three-quarter sky. It can be dark and unwelcoming or it is bathed with incandescent light to arouse emotion in the most insensitive of people. Mountains and hills have their own interpretation of radiant beauty but daylight there does not last as long as in the Fens. Here the sun sinks to the horizon much later and produces sunsets of indescribable colour. To don wellingtons and stand on the flooded washland is fulfilment in a spiritual sense. The moment comes when colour overwhelms the horizon and, caught by the water, it reflects to the point where you stand. It is transformed into a sparkling red, orange and gold iridescence quite out of this world. This is what the ancient Fenmen marvelled at as they followed the bells' sound and made their way back to the islands.

Strangers visiting the Fens for the first time and seeing the flooded washland believe what they are beholding is a disaster. But no! The deliberate flooding is part of the plan conceived more than 300 years ago to save the land from drowning. Spectacular sunsets and sunrises compliment mens achievements in an area where Fen dwellers ought to be up to their necks in water. It is harmony between man and nature.

Charles Kingsley, a great admirer of the Fens, had this to say:

'The Fens have a beauty of their own, a beauty as of the sea, of boundless expanse and freedom. Overhead the arch of heaven spreads more ample than elsewhere, as over the open sea, and that vastness gave and still gives such cloud banks, such sunrises, such sunsets as can be seen nowhere else in these isles.'

Three Fenmen of Note

Immortalised by Charles Kingsley, Hereward the Wake ascends the pinnacle of fame in a well told romantic story by a masterful story teller.

Many have referred to the exploits of Hereward, warrior of the Fens as pure myth, but sufficient evidence does exist on the man, a rebel cast away from his father's estate at Bourne. Hereward became a valued mercenary much in demand in Ireland and in the Netherlands.

Stories galore have been told of his adventures, but it was in the Fens, principally the Isle of Ely, that his cunning and military prowess ranged against a man of equal ability whose aim was to conquer all England. It was in the Fens, four years after the Battle of Hastings, that William the Conqueror was finally held at bay for the best part of a year by insurgents led by Hereward the Saxon.

Two reliable chroniclers, Hugh Candidus of Peterborough and Robert of Ely, writing about their respective abbeys, made significant investigation of the siege of the Isle of Ely and Hereward's exploits, making use of documents written a few years before their time outlining the distinguished siege in the swamps and higher ground of the Isle.

It was recorded that Hugh Candidus wrote the truth but he was not an admirer of Hereward who ordered Danish allies to carry away treasure from Gildenburgh

(Peterborough) abbey to prevent King William from seizing it. In doing so the Danes created great havoc and severely damaged a number of monastery buildings.

De Gestis Herwardi Saxonis is mostly the work of Robert of Ely. It states that former soldiers led by Hereward were, in times of peace, invited by chroniclers to the monastery to relate accounts of the man and his epic battle against the King. Hugh Candidus wrote: *'I write of nothing and I speak of nothing save that which I found recorded in the writings of old time, or heard from the lips of faithful witnesses'*. The famous siege of Ely is mentioned by several old time chroniclers.

Matthew Paris, compiler of the *Chronica Majora* in the 13th century mentions the Isle of Ely where the Anglo-Saxon nobility, smarting from their defeat at Hastings, sought refuge in the years following the Battle of Hastings. These men organised resistance against the King but they lacked a suitable leader. Hereward, incensed at his brother's murder by Normans that had seized his father's estate, was chosen to lead the resistance from the Isle of Ely. The abbot of Ely acted as an uneasy host and plans were made to harass the Conqueror at every given opportunity.

The Battle of Hastings in 1066 was narrowly won by the Norman invaders in a day, but at least four years passed before the King could claim to have taken England completely. The resistance from the Isle of Ely alarmed him and he later admitted that Hereward and his prowess as a leader and in battle was a man after his own heart and worthy of praise. The King's greatest fear was that the ongoing resistance in the Fens could break out and affect the whole of the country.

King William organised a number of assaults upon the insurgents who, familiar with the marshy ground, thwarted every attempt. Hundreds of Norman soldiers perished. In the end King William stationed almost three-quarters of his army around the Fen perimeter to prevent the rebels from breaking out.

It is thought the King attempted to cross the marsh from Stuntney where burnt timber, probably an old causeway, was found. A more favourable route for him was from near Willingham across the marsh to Aldreth, near Haddenham. Chroniclers recorded that the Conqueror's men, fully armed, almost succeeded in crossing the treacherous marsh using inflated cow hides to support them. Waiting for the Normans, Hereward and his men set fire to oil poured on the water and fired a mass of arrows towards them. In the panic to escape the arrows and flames, men jumped into the water and most, weighed down by chain mail, drowned.

Norman knights were astonished when a captured knight, released by Hereward, explained he had dined with the insurgents at Ely monastery. He told them that the insurgents lived extraordinarily well on produce from the Isle and lacked nothing. On the walls of the refectory hung weapons of all kinds and shields and, most amazing of all, some of the monks were skilled in warfare and could arm themselves in a thrice. A chronicler recorded that some had, in fact, taken part in a skirmish at Burwell. In the knight's opinion, the King would do well to make peace with the insurgents.

In the end, the abbot, growing weary of the siege, asked the King for terms.

> 'They made arrangements for the King to come at once and secretly to the Isle when Hereward had gone with his men foraging, in order that the affair might be managed without bloodshed and grievous slaughter'.

Hereward, livid at this betrayal, threatened to set fire to the abbey but was persuaded by a monk to leave. For a time he survived as a fugitive in the Wide Sea, a lake in the Fens. Eventually he, and several of his followers, escaped to Northamptonshire where he conducted resistance for a time and kidnapped abbot Turold of Peterborough, released on payment of a substantial ransom.

The *De Gestis Herwardi* goes on to relate that after Hereward had divorced his wife Turfrida, he married a wealthy Anglo-Saxon woman which, he later admitted, was a mistake. The King, seeing a stroke of fortune in these events by which peace could be made, declared he would like to see Hereward in person and receive him in his favour.

William the Conqueror visited Hereward and his unarmed soldiers and they paraded before him. The King, it is written, was delighted and ranked his former enemies as the greatest soldiers he had seen. They then went away to their houses and Hereward received his father's estate from the Conqueror. From then on Hereward *faithfully served the King and wholly devoted to his family and friends'*.

CROMWELL AND HIS FIGHTING FENMEN

Born at Huntingdon on the edge of the Fens, Oliver Cromwell had a passionate feeling for the flatland and its people. The Civil War introduced him to the heartiness of the Fenmen and much of his political career centred on his farming experiences and the grasping attitudes of the ruling class, exemplified by Charles I.

When Cromwell lay aside his sickle and took up the sword, he cleaved a path through the hollows of depression burdening the citizens of a nation chronically sick at heart. Its sharp edge thrust deep into the bowels of royal prerogative. At the end of it all the man that wielded it wrote: *'He that ventures his life for the liberty of his country, I wish he trust God for the liberty of his conscience and for the liberty he fights for.'*

It was inevitable that imposition by royal decree hanging round the necks of countrymen and townsmen alike would finally be rejected by a man born for the part. Oliver Cromwell was that man. Though he did not realise it, his destiny was the Ship of State and he drew its original crew from the Fens.

Cromwell's severity towards extreme enactments made him enemies. Some church buildings did suffer at the hands of Puritan soldiers, but the same can be said of the Royalists who had fortified the buildings. Cromwell himself ordered that property and goods be respected but civil war is the worst of wars and looting of shops and houses did take place. The Isle of Ely formed a strongpoint for the Eastern Counties Association, the nerve centre of the Parliamentary cause. Small fortresses were erected at Earith, March and Wisbech and a troop of fifty horse stationed at March patrolled the Fens and displayed their flag to discourage Royalist sympathisers.

The Fens' greatest contribution to Parliament's campaign was the formation of horse and foot whose fighting abilities were without parallel. It was in the Fens that the New Model Army had its beginning, resolute yeomen leaving the fields and dykes, bidding farewell to their families and taking up muskets and swords. In barns and broad spaces they learned a new art of war which was to change the nation forever. It is said that Cromwell used a barn at St. Ives in connection with his farming interests and for training the first group of highly disciplined troops who would form the embryo of the New Model Army. Unfortunately the barn associated with the world's greatest cavalry officer was demolished years ago.

So what did Oliver Cromwell think of his russet-coated Fen warriors?

'I raised such men as had the fear of God before them and made some conscience of what they did. And from that day forward they were never beaten, but wherever they were engaged against the enemy they beat continually.'

Since the times of William the Conqueror, the Isle of Ely inspired men with an emboldened vision of freedom. It was the last area in the country to submit to the Norman invaders. Neither did it did lack the will to fight for freedom of the nation's beleaguered countrymen when civil war broke upon the nation, and its own son Oliver Cromwell restored England to a pinnacle of greatness.

Cromwell's strength lay in his determination to abolish the divine right of kings to govern wrong. His Ironsides followed him with Spartan firmness and gave England the embryo of a modern army. They developed the cult of professional soldiers and their prowess on the battlefield swept all before them. When they fought they sounded the liberty bell for unborn generations. Here in the Fens the Commonwealth had its beginning.

Despite his failing to persuade the king to re-occupy the throne conditionally, Oliver Cromwell can be credited for establishing constitutional monarchy. It is ever to the shame of the country that, after the Restoration, his body was torn from its resting place and beheaded, purely an act of vengeance in the name of the 'Merry Monarch' whose example signalled the land to indulge once again in weak and immoral practices.

Oliver Cromwell's real worth is measured in the services to his country. One should look no further than to compare England under him than England under Charles II.

Ship Owner Extraordinaire

Ely, spiritual bastion of the Fens, honours great churchmen in their own right, acclaimed architects and even a bishop-cum-drainage engineer. March is proud of a church with an internationally acclaimed angel roof of outstanding beauty. Wisbech is associated with Thomas Clarkson of anti-slavery fame and Octavia Hill, fighter for social reform. Another worthy emerged from modest beginnings into the field of opportunism and was highly successful in the port's commercial achievements.

He was Richard Young, born at Scarning, Norfolk in 1809. In 1830, Young was appointed superintendent of the Nene Outfall works and became keeper of the North Level sluice, an office he held for 30 years. He was MP for Cambridgeshire and Sheriff of London and Middlesex in addition to being appointed JP for the Isle of Ely and elected five times as Mayor of Wisbech. Two days after being elected Sheriff of London and Middlesex at the City Guildhall on October 15th, 1871 he died.

At one time Richard Young was a gardener at Wisbech but gave this up to follow his instincts at Wisbech port which then had no fewer than fifty master mariners. He purchased a share in a small trading vessel and succeeded in accumulating handsome profits, enabling him to purchase a brig, the *Tycho Wing*. The vessel had been built at Wisbech by Mr Cousins, shipbuilder. The sail ship was the largest of its kind at Wisbech and it was not unusual in the 1850s to see thirty such vessels moored at the docks.

Young commissioned the local shipbuilder to construct a barque, a large vessel, named after him. Thoroughly immersed in shipping, he built Osborn House overlooking the River Nene. Sailing ships were beginning to give way to steam ships and Young ordered a handsome ship, the *Lady Alice Lambton,* Wisbech port's first screw steamer of 700 tons. The vessel was built at a port in the north and carried two guns. As it entered Wisbech port for the first time, its guns fired a salute.

The Wisbech magnate contributed in no small manner to the ancient borough where shipbuilding and renovating was an important part of the town's trade. On one occasion Young organised an excursion on the *Lady Alice Lambton* and it carried eight hundred people to the mouth of the Humber. He eventually owned a large fleet of iron steam ships and sailing vessels. During the Crimean War his ship *The Great Northern* was chartered and sailed to the Crimea carrying several local working men with tools and materials to construct fortifications. Young sold the steamer *Sir Colin Campbell,* soon after it was launched, to the Turkish government. The government renamed it *Rechid Pasha* and it was used as a troop carrier. After the war Mr Young re-purchased it at highly advantageous terms. Some of Richard Young's ships were chartered by the British government for conveying supplies to the army in foreign places. All this placed the Wisbech tycoon in a sound financial position. His demise at the age of sixty-two was a great blow to Wisbech and the port in particular, for which he worked tirelessly and determinedly.

SUGGESTED FURTHER READING

Bevis, Trevor. 1991. *Flooded Fens.* Published by the author
Bevis, Trevor. 1992. *Water, Water Everywhere.* Published by the author
Bevis, Trevor. 1999. *The River Makers.* Published by the author
Bevis, Trevor. 2003. *Prisoners of the Fens.* Published by the author
Gardiner, F. J. 1898. *History of Wisbech and Neighbourhood 1848-1898.* Gardiner & Co
Gerrard, Valerie. 2003. *The Story of the Fens.* Robert Hale, London
Storey, Edward. 1996. *In Fen Country Heaven.* Robert Hale, London
Wells, Samuel. 2 vols. 1830. *History of the Great Level of the Fens.* Published by the author
History, Gazetter and Directory of Cambridgeshire. (Robert Gardner 1850)

This title is one in a new series by **Cottage Publications**.
For more information and to see our other titles, please visit our website
www.cottage-publications.com
or alternatively you can contact us as follows:–

Telephone: +44 (0)28 9188 8033
Fax: +44 (0)28 9188 8063

Cottage Publications
is an imprint of
Laurel Cottage Ltd.,
15 Ballyhay Road,
Donaghadee, Co. Down,
N. Ireland, BT21 0NG